Jazz Suite No. 3
for Clarinet, Cajón, and Piano

BY GLENDA AUSTIN

ISBN 978-1-5400-7251-1

WILLIS MUSIC

EXCLUSIVELY DISTRIBUTED BY

HAL•LEONARD®

Contact us:
Hal Leonard
7777 West Bluemound Road
Milwaukee, WI 53213
Email: info@halleonard.com

In Europe, contact:
Hal Leonard Europe Limited
42 Wigmore Street
Marylebone, London, W1U 2RN
Email: info@halleonardeurope.com

In Australia, contact:
Hal Leonard Australia Pty. Ltd.
4 Lentara Court
Cheltenham, Victoria, 3192 Australia
Email: info@halleonard.com.au

FROM THE COMPOSER

I am honored that the Music Teachers National Association commissioned me to write a piece promoting collaborative performance. The instruments selected for 2020 were piano, clarinet, and cajón. They presented a pleasing challenge, and one that proved to be quite gratifying! Thus, *Jazz Suite No. 3* was born. In each of the three contrasting movements, an instrument is highlighted: 1st movement – piano, 2nd movement – clarinet, and 3rd movement – cajón.

It is with much gratitude that I thank Ann Rivers Witherspoon (MTNA Chair of Composer Commissioning) for the distinct opportunity to be part of *From Pen to Premiere*. On a personal note, the performers at the premiere: Janice Wenger (piano), Wesley Warnhoff (clarinet), and Julia Gaines (cajón) are all faculty members at the University of Missouri at Columbia, which is my alma mater. I am a very proud alumna – go Tigers!

Jazz Suite No. 3 is also available as a piano solo, and it is my hope that teachers and students will welcome this piece to their repertoire.

All the best,

Glenda Austin

March 22, 2020
Chicago, Illinois

CONTENTS

Jazz Suite No. 3

Glenda Austin

* Cajón player may improvise, as desired.

III. Intriguing and mysterious ♩ = 112–120

* Play detached throughout unless indicated.

Jazz Suite No. 3

Clarinet in B♭

Glenda Austin

II. Freely flowing, with flexibility

III. Intriguing and mysterious ♩ = 112–120

Jazz Suite No. 3

Cajón

Glenda Austin

II. Freely flowing, with flexibility ♩ = 76–88 ♫ = ♫

III. Intriguing and mysterious ♩ = 112–120